Queen Alexandra's Christmas Gift Book

University of Toronto

Joseph Burr Tyrrell

Graduate of the University of Toronto,
and Canadian geologist,
author, and writer

QUEEN ALEXANDRA'S CHRISTMAS GIFT BOOK

PHOTOGRAPHS FROM MY CAMERA

*To be Sold
for Charity*

PUBLISHED BY
" THE DAILY TELEGRAPH "
LONDON
1908

The King at Balmoral.

The King, May,
Lady Katherine Coke and Captain Welch.

The King at Balmoral.

The King, May,
Lady Katherine Coke and Captain Welsh.

The King
returning for Lunch from a Deer Drive.

The King,
Sir Dighton Probyn and Sir Henry Knollys.

Party at Balmoral.

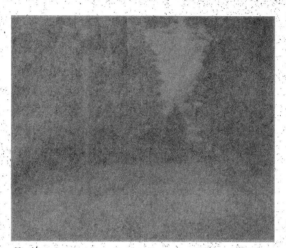

The King.
returning for Lunch from a Deer Drive.

The King.
Sir Dighton Probyn and Sir Henry Knollys.

Party at Balmoral.

Arthur Connaught,
Mr Hervey and May.

My Two Grandsons wading.

Victoria
and Captain Welsh

Sir A. Davidson and General Sir D. Probyn.

Fishing Party at Loch Muick.

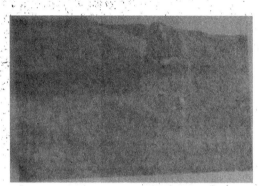

Castle Garden in Scotland.

The interior of Castle

Group at Balmoral.

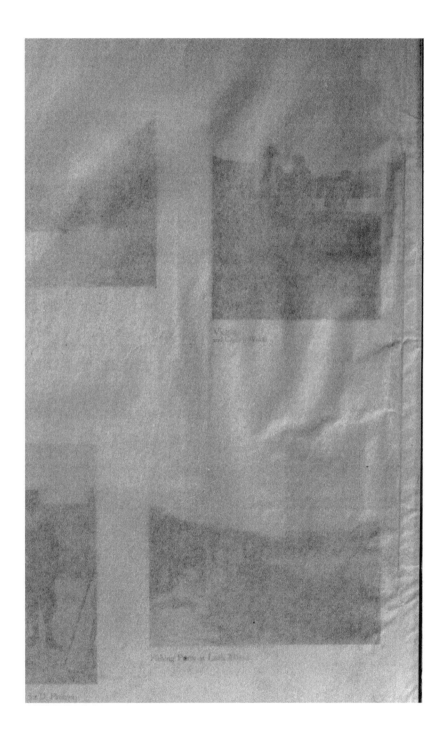

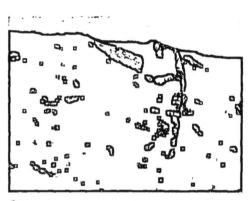

Cameron
fishing with me in Scotland

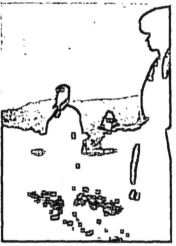

The Piper Cameron and Victoria.

Duchesse d'Aosta
and Colonel Henry Knollys.

Group at Balmoral.

Shooting Party : Duke of Connaught,
his son, Count de Benckendorff, Sir M. de Bunsen,
and Sir C. Hardinge.

Princess of Wales
and Duchesse d'Aosta.

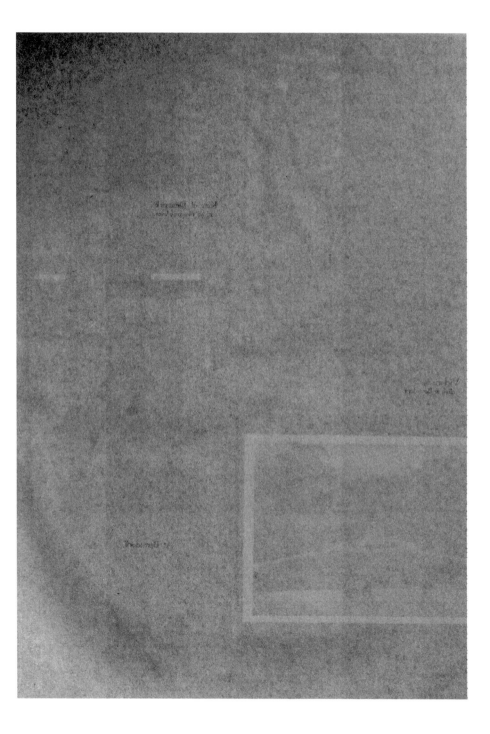

King of Denmark
and his two grandsons.

Shooting Party: Duke of Connaught,
his son, Count de Beuckendorff, Sir M. de Bunsen,
and Sir C. Hardinge.

Victoria
riding at Bernsdorff.

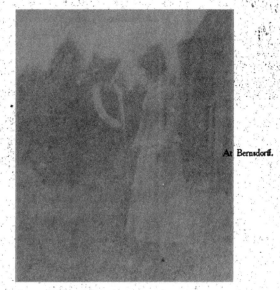

At Bernsdorff.

Princess of Wales
and Duchess d'Aosta.

Sandringham.

Sandringham.

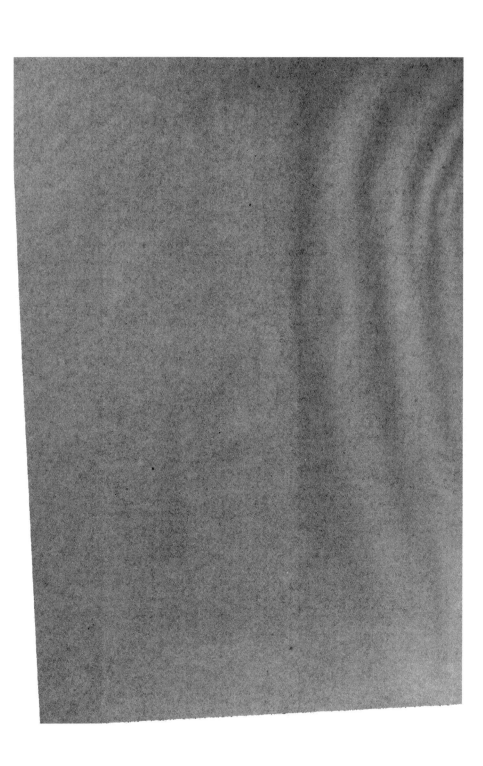

Sandringham.

Sandringham.

Wilton House, Salisbury.

Wilton tea-party:
Lord and Lady Lansdowne, Lady de Grey,
and Lord Pembroke.

The Thames—Boulter's Lock.

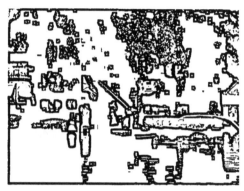

The Club at Maidenhead.

On the River.

In the Lock.

The King and Emperor
off Reval.

Ольга,   Татьяна Анастасія, Марія.

Марія

The Mother, Sister, and Children
of the Emperor of Russia.

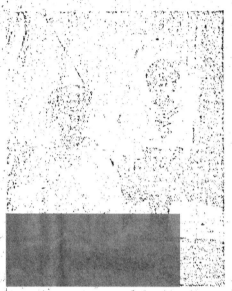

The little Cassarstitch
with his Sailor French.

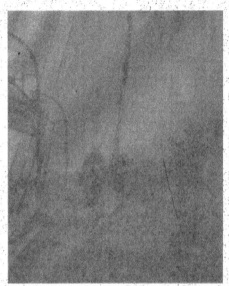

The King and Emperor
of China.

Olga, *Tatiana Romanoff, M.*

Alexis

The Mother, Sister, and Children
of the Emperor of Russia.

The little Cæsarevitch
with his Sailor Friend. Деревенко дядепько и маленький Алексей

Мари,　　　Татьяна Анастасия

The Emperor's children and Victoria.

Reval.

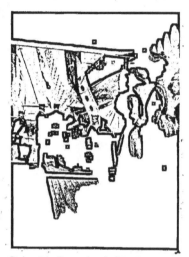

On board the Emperor's yacht "Standart."
The young Empress and Victoria.

Sir Charles Hardinge, Sir Arthur Nicolson
and General Sir John French.

Empress of Russia
at Hvidöre.

Empress of Russia
and her son Michael
at Hvidöre.

Empress of Russia.
Danish Ships off Hvidöre.

0

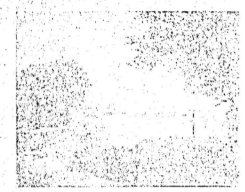

Hvidsten.—Danish Gunboats
during Manœuvres under Prince Waldemar.

Copenhagen.—
Group on board.

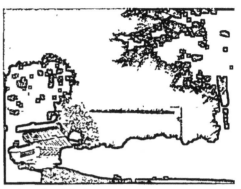

Hvidōre.—Danish Gunboats
during Manœuvres under Prince Waldemar

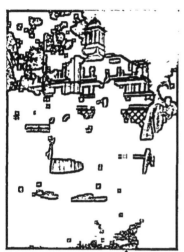

Hvidōre. *Auaemaer* *Danemark*

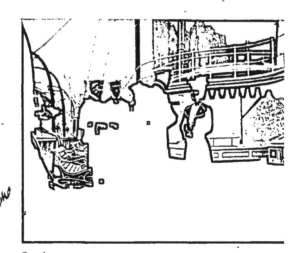

Copenhagen.—
Group on board

At Bygdö —
Charles, little Olav and Victoria.

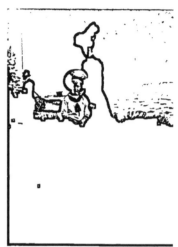

Maud and little Olav
at Bygdö.

Charles and little Olav.

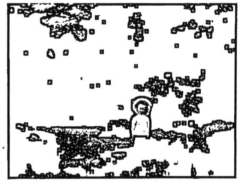

Little Olav,
Bygdö.

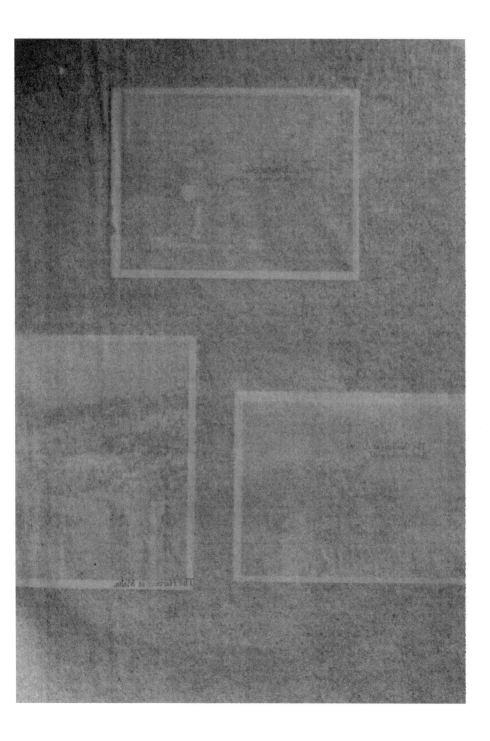

Duke of Sparta
in his garden at Athens.

At Phaleron.
Charles and Prince Nicholas.

Mixed and little Olav
at Spala.

The Stadium at Athens
(built of white marble).

The Harbour at Malta.

Charles and little Olav.

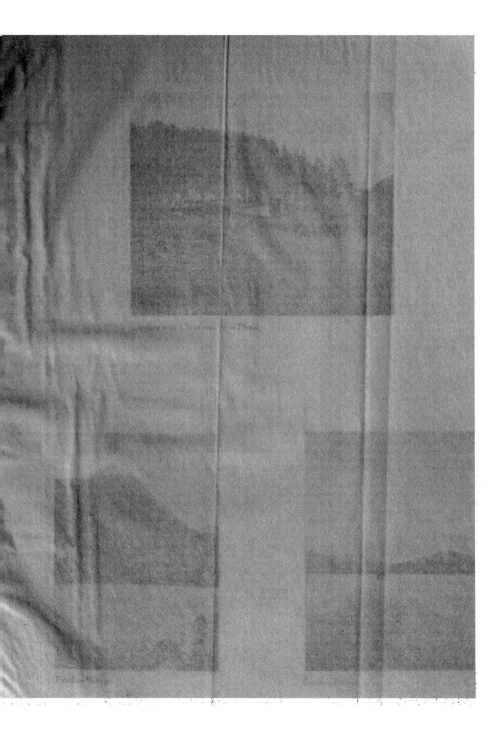

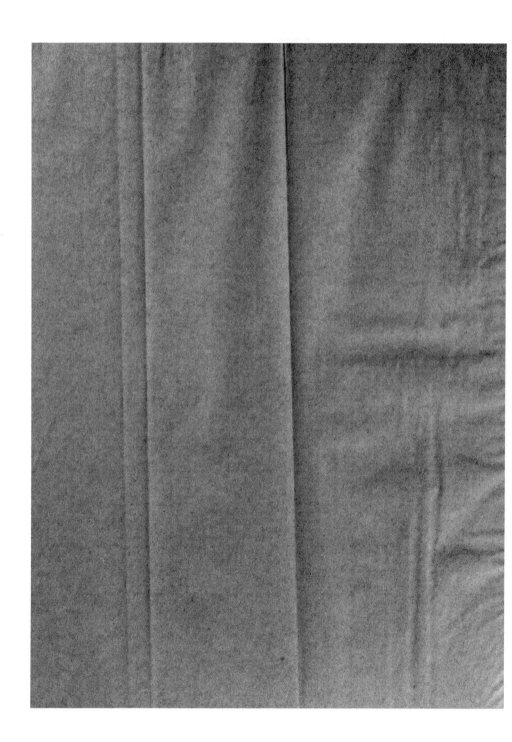

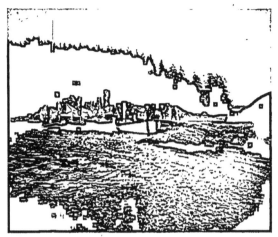

Landing near Christiania for a Picnic.

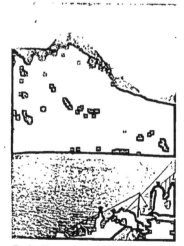

Fiords—Norway

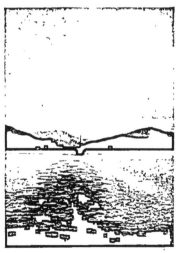

Fiords—Norway

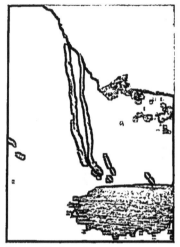

Norway.—The Seven Sisters

" Victoria and Albert "
at Christiania

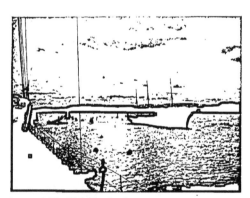

Norway.—The " Polar Star " at Sunset

Professor Tuxen's house

Victoria
and little Olav.
Mediterranean, 1905.

Norway.—The Seven Sisters.

Miss Knollys and Lady Antrim.
Little Olav.

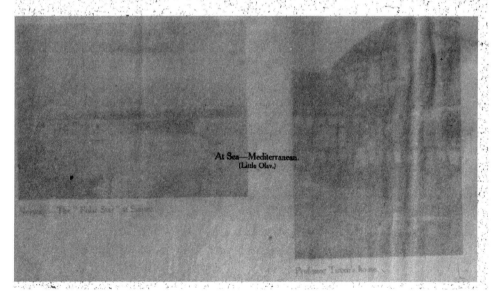

At Sea—Mediterranean.
(Little Olav.)

Group on board.
Christiania.

Group on board.
Christiania.

Group on board,
Christiania.

Group on board,
Christiania.

My brother George of Greece and
Chevalier Martino, at the Empress of Austria's Villa,
"Achilles," Corfu.

At Corfu.

"The Dying Achilles"
in the Garden of the Empress of Austria's Villa, Corfu.

At Corfu.

Our Treasury of ... of Cuba

Iy brother George of Greece and
brother Ivan ho, at the Empress of Austria's Villa,
Achilles," Corfu.

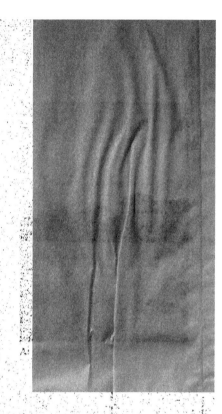

A

"The Dying Achilles"
the Garden of the Empress of Austria's Villa, Corfu.

At Corfu.

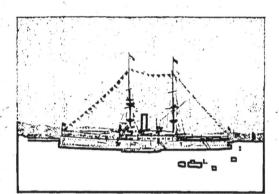

Return of the Prince of Wales from India.
The "Renown" at Corfu.

Our Tea-party at Monrepos, Corfu.

Edward R.I.

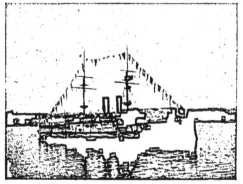

Escort of the Prince of Wales from India.

Corfu   My brother George,
Commodore Keppel and Lord Howe.

Our Escort—1906.

H M S. "Essex"

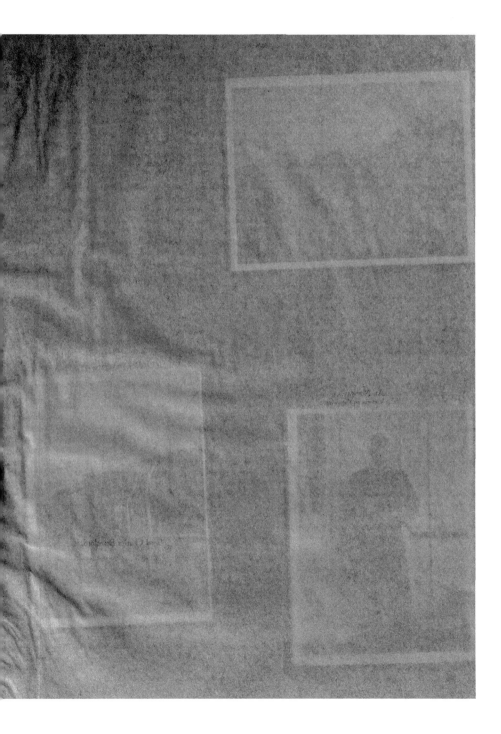

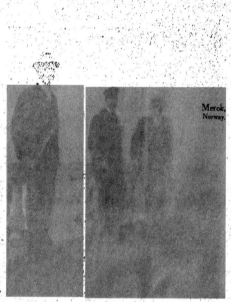

Merok,
Norway.

Corfu. My brother C...
Commodore Keppel and ...

At Norway.
Victoria on the swing.

Our Eight—1906.

Lord Charles Beresford.

Opening of the Alexandra Dock,
Cardiff, 1907.

Naval Review
off Portsmouth.

Commodore Sir B. Milne.

"The Nimrod" (Captain Shackleton)
going to the South Pole (1907)

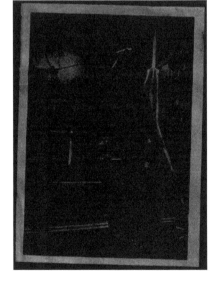

CPSIA information can be obtained
at www.ICGtesting.com
Printed in the USA
BVHW010107111021
618631BV00002BA/7